U for what?

My Kid Words Series (Book U)

Learn 30 Words Starting with Letter U and Learn Little Information about those Words.

U for Umbrella

An umbrella or parasol is a folding canopy supported by wooden or metal ribs that is usually mounted on a wooden, metal, or plastic pole. It is designed to protect a person against rain or sunlight.

U for Unicycle

A unicycle is a vehicle that touches the ground with only one wheel. The most common variation has a frame with a saddle and has a pedal-driven direct-drive. A two-speed hub is commercially available for faster unicycling.

U for Utensils

A utensil is a tool you can hold in your hand and use around the house. In the kitchen, common utensils are the knives, forks, and spoons that we hold in our hands and use to eat.

U for USB drive

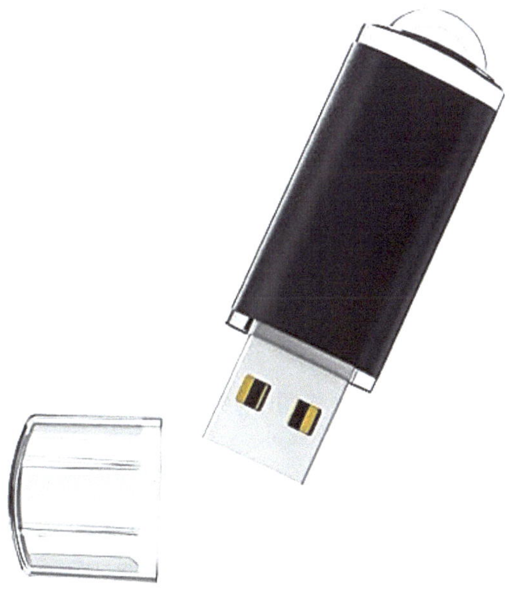

A USB drive, also referred to as a flash drive or memory stick, is a small, portable device that plugs into the USB port on your computer. USB drives are commonly used for storage, data backup, and transferring files between devices.

U for U boat

A U-boat is a military submarine used by Germany. German submarines were most active in the First Battle of the Atlantic in World War I and in World War II. The typical U-boat was 214 feet long, carried 35 men and 12 torpedoes, and could travel underwater for two hours at a time.

U for Utility vehicle

A utility vehicle is a vehicle, generally motorized, that is designed to carry out a specific task with more efficacy than a passenger vehicle. It sometimes refers to a small truck with low sides.

U for Urinal

A urinal is a special-purpose toilet, made only for urinating by males in public restrooms.

U for Urn

An urn is a vase, often with a cover, with a typically narrowed neck above a rounded body and a footed pedestal.

U for Ursinia

The genus ursinia is part of the asteraceae botanical family and contains around 40 flowering plant species that grow as annuals, herbaceous perennials, and sometimes as small sub shrubs as well. This plant is more commonly known as the orange African daisy, the Namawaka daisy, or the glossy eyed parachute daisy.

U for Ugli fruit

Ugli fruit, also known as Jamaican tangelo or uniq fruit, is a cross between an orange and a grapefruit. It's gaining popularity for its novelty and sweet, citrusy taste. People also like it because it's easy to peel.

U for Unicorn

The unicorn is a imaginary animal that looks like a horse or a goat with a single horn on its forehead. Unicorns are thought to be good and pure creatures with magical powers. They are strong, often white in color, and difficult to catch.

U for Urial

Urial also known as the arkars or shapo is an upland wild sheep of southern and central Asia which is reddish brown and the males of which have a beard from the neck to the chest.

U for Uakari

Uakari is any of several types of short-tailed South American monkeys with shaggy fur, humanlike ears, and distinctive bald faces that become flushed when the animal is excited. In two of the three color forms, the face is bright red.

U for Ural owl

Ural owls have an extremely broad distribution. It extends as far west as much of Scandinavia, montane eastern Europe, and, sporadically, central Europe through Russia to as far east as Sakhalin and throughout Japan. This nocturnal bird is named after the Ural Mountains, generally considered to be a dividing line between Europe and Asia.

U for Umbrella bird

An umbrella bird is about the same size as a crow and loves to eat large insects and spiders. They also eat frogs, lizards, and small birds. Their large curved beaks help them to pick fruit and berries from the treetops. They are named for their distinct umbrella-like hoods.

U for Unicornfish

T

he unicornfish is easily identified by the bony horn on its forehead, in front of the eyes, though not all species exhibit this horn. The unicornfish does not use its horn for defense, but rather its sharp tail spines. Biologists are unsure of the purpose of the horn.

U for Uncle

Someone's uncle is the brother of their mother or father, or the husband of their aunt.

U for Uniform

Uniforms are special clothes to show that a group of people belong together. The group of people will all be dressed in the same way. People may wear uniforms for several reasons.

U for University

A university is an institution of higher education, usually comprising a college of liberal arts and sciences and graduate and professional schools and having the authority to confer degrees in various fields of study.

U for United State

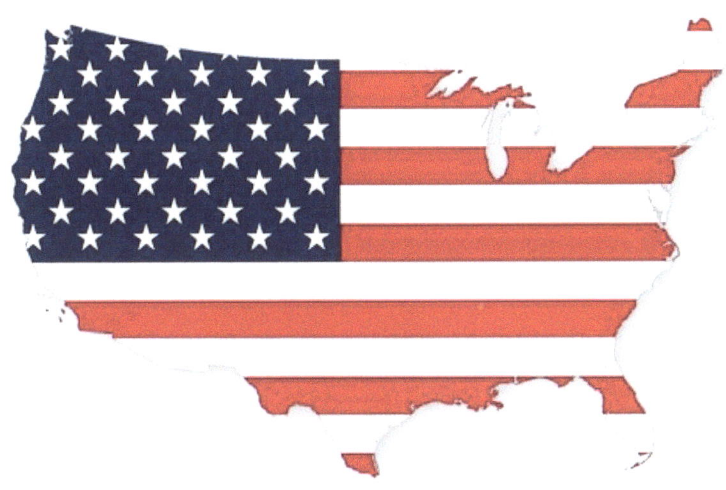

The United States of America is the world's third largest country in size and nearly the third largest in terms of population. Located in North America, the country is bordered on the west by the Pacific Ocean and to the east by the Atlantic Ocean. Along the northern border is Canada and the southern border is Mexico.

U for United Kingdom

United Kingdom is an island country spanning an archipelago including Great Britain, located in Western Europe comprising England, Scotland, Wales, and Northern Ireland. United Kingdom is surrounded by the Atlantic Ocean, the North Sea, the English Channel, and the Irish Sea.

U for U-turn

A U-turn in driving refers to performing a 180° rotation to reverse the direction of travel. A turn made by a car in order to go back in the direction from which it has come: It is illegal to do/make a U-turn on a motorway.

U for Ugly

Ugly means very unattractive or unpleasant to look at; offensive to the sense of beauty; displeasing in appearance.

U for Upset

Upset means is someone is worried, unhappy, or angry.

U for Undertaker

Undertaker is a person whose business is preparing dead bodies for burial or cremation and making arrangements for funerals.

U for Underground

Underground is the beneath the surface of the earth. Most rabbit species in the wild live in underground burrows that they dig.

U for Underwater

Underwater is a term telling what is below the surface of a body of water such as an ocean, sea, lake, pond, or river. Most of the planet Earth is covered by water. The bottom of the ocean is called the sea-bed. Most of the sea-bed is between 4,000 and 5,500 meters (13,100 and 18,000 ft) below the surface of the ocean.

U for UFO

UFO stands for unidentified flying objects. They are sometimes also referred to as unidentified aerial phenomena, or UAP. Some people believe that sightings of UFOs and UAPs are evidence of extraterrestrial intelligence.

U for Uranus

Uranus is an ice giant (instead of a gas giant). It is mostly made of flowing icy materials above a solid core. Uranus has a thick atmosphere made of methane, hydrogen, and helium. Uranus is the only planet that spins on its side. Uranus spins the opposite direction as Earth and most other planets. The closest Uranus can get to Earth is 2.57 billion km (1.6 billion miles).

U for Universe

The Universe is everything we can touch, feel, sense, measure or detect. It includes living things, planets, stars, galaxies, dust clouds, light, and even time. Before the birth of the Universe, time, space and matter did not exist. While the spatial size of the entire universe is unknown, it is possible to measure the size of the observable universe, which is approximately 93 billion light-years in diameter at the present day.

Check out other books in this series·